Well-behaved women seldom make history.
—LAUREL THATCHER ULRICH

Mary Todd Lincoln

KATHLEEN KRULL

interior illustrations by
Elizabeth Baddeley

BLOOMSBURY
NEW YORK   LONDON   NEW DELHI   SYDNEY

To Robin Hansen,

a woman who really breaks the rules

Text copyright © 2015 by Kathleen Krull
Interior illustrations copyright © 2015 by Elizabeth Baddeley
Cover illustration copyright © 2015 by Edwin Fotheringham

First published in the United States of America in December 2015
by Bloomsbury Children's Books
www.bloomsbury.com

Bloomsbury is a registered trademark of Bloomsbury Publishing Plc

For information about permission to reproduce selections from this book, write to
Permissions, Bloomsbury Children's Books, 1385 Broadway, New York, New York 10018
Bloomsbury books may be purchased for business or promotional use. For information on bulk purchases please contact
Macmillan Corporate and Premium Sales Department at specialmarkets@macmillan.com

Library of Congress Cataloging-in-Publication Data
Krull, Kathleen.
Women who broke the rules : Mary Todd Lincoln / by Kathleen Krull ; illustrated by Elizabeth Baddeley.
pages   cm
ISBN 978-0-8027-3825-7 (paperback) • ISBN 978-0-8027-3824-0 (hardcover)
1. Lincoln, Mary Todd, 1818–1882—Juvenile literature. 2. Presidents' spouses—United States—Biography—
Juvenile literature. I. Baddeley, Elizabeth, illustrator. II. Title. III. Title: Mary Todd Lincoln.
E457.25.L55K78 2014   973.7092—dc23   [B]   2014032451

Art created with mixed media
Typeset in Beaufort
Book design by Nicole Gastonguay

Printed in China by Leo Paper Products, Heshan, Guangdong
2 4 6 8 10 9 7 5 3 1 (paperback)
2 4 6 8 10 9 7 5 3 1 (hardcover)

All papers used by Bloomsbury Publishing, Inc., are natural, recyclable products
made from wood grown in well-managed forests. The manufacturing processes
conform to the environmental regulations of the country of origin.

TABLE OF CONTENTS

1 DRAMA QUEEN

Mary Todd had a great brain. But that wasn't always a comfort. America in the 1800s, with its narrow ideas about women, just didn't know what to do with her.

She was born on December 13, 1818, in Lexington, Kentucky. Her parents were rich and important. Her family had founded Lexington, a polished Southern city with one horrible flaw—its slave trade.

Whatever Mary wanted—even her own pony—she got. She went fishing for minnows, sewed stylish clothes for her dolls, and romped with her cousins and many siblings.

Said one cousin, "She was always playing pranks, and was the fearless and inventive leader in every possible kind of mischief."

It wasn't hard to read her moods: "Her face was an index to every passing emotion," said the cousin.

She was, in short, a drama queen.

It was a painful blow to six-year-old Mary when her mother died. Even worse was that her father quickly remarried. In her first lecture to Mary and her sisters, the new stepmother said, "It takes seven generations to make a lady. You are six generations short."

Mary got back at her by doing things like putting salt in her coffee. Her stepmother took to calling Mary "a limb of Satan," and soon the other Todds were teasing her with this nickname.

The Todd family eventually included sixteen children. So how was Mary to get the attention she craved? One way was to sit in on her father's political chats with his male friends. He encouraged her to read the newspaper, and she was able to pipe up with comments about slavery and who was running for president.

Most girls got fewer than four years of education (in manners, cooking, and sewing), but Mary's father decided to give Mary as much schooling as she wanted.

So at age eight she went off to an elite academy for girls. Neighbors watched her zipping the three blocks to the school each day, as if she couldn't get there fast enough. She loved her classes in math, philosophy, geography, and science. A friend said she was "far in advance over the other girls" with "a fine mind that enabled her to grasp and understand thoroughly."

At fourteen she enrolled in boarding school. The director was a brilliant, independent Frenchwoman whom Mary took on as a role model. She learned to speak French and studied dance, drama, poetry, music, and more.

By sixteen, Mary was calling slavery "a monstrous wrong." She'd worried about it for years, educating herself on the topic, debating her family—all odd behavior for a girl of her time and place. From Sally, the slave who took care of her, she learned that her own house was a stop on the Underground Railroad. This highly illegal system helped runaway slaves escape. Sally trusted Mary to keep the secret and help out, which she did.

Being a brain broke the rules for women in her day. Mary was "the most ambitious woman I ever knew," said her sister. College wasn't an option. Yet Mary was set on making her mark. What great deeds could she do?

Not very much, as far as she could tell, except attach herself to a great man. She did like to brag about something *really* odd—how she planned to marry a president one day.

2 NO ORDINARY HOUSEWIFE

At twenty, Mary was a belle of the ball living with her sister in Springfield, Illinois. She went horseback riding and mastered the polka, the waltz, and all the latest dances. Her razor-sharp wit brightened tea parties and late-night dinners. She debated current events with her many suitors. If they couldn't keep up, she mocked them right to their faces.

Abraham Lincoln had never met anyone like her. He was a lawyer, brilliant but struggling, active in local politics, and kind of a dork around women. His first words to her were "Miss Todd, I want to dance with you in the worst way."

She wasn't put off by his awkward manners (not to mention his bad dancing). And *he* wasn't put off by her brain. They talked for hours about poetry and politics. He was a good listener and respected her opinions. He could even make her laugh. To get around his awkwardness, Lincoln had a store of jokes and stories, keeping them G-rated when ladies were present.

Years ahead of his time, Lincoln thought women should have the right to vote. Like most in her day, Mary deemed voting "unwomanly." But this man certainly was a breath of fresh air.

True, Lincoln had rough edges. And Mary was just the woman to smooth them.

They became engaged. Then, in one of history's mysteries, they broke up. One factor might have been her family's objections that he wasn't good enough for her. A year and a half passed, a miserable time for both of them, though she continued with her parties and picnics.

Finally a friend put them in the same room and said, "Be friends again." They started talking politics . . . and were married on November 4, 1842.

She was twenty-three years old, he was thirty-three, and they were total opposites. His manners were crude (eating peas with his butter knife when he used silverware at all); hers were elegant. She had a superior education; he had one year of formal schooling. He towered fourteen inches over her. He couldn't care less about his clothes; she obsessed over every detail. He was silent and calm; she was chatty and emotional.

But they were devoted to each other, looked forward to raising children together, and had ambitions: "He is to be

President of the United States some day," she wrote a friend; "if I had not thought so, I never would have married him, for you can see he is not pretty."

In their room at a boardinghouse, they laughed often. He put on the black velvet slippers she'd embroidered with his initials, and she read the newspaper aloud to him.

After their first two beloved boys, Robert and Edward, were born, and Lincoln's career took off, they were able to buy a small five-room house.

Mary was now a housewife. She worked from morning until night, sometimes with hired neighborhood girls to help.

She cooked everything from scratch—if she wanted fried chicken, she had to kill the chicken and pluck its feathers first. She milked the cow, shopped, made almost all their clothes, hauled wood, gardened, did laundry, and cleaned.

Where was Lincoln? He did help out, especially with childcare, much more than the average husband. But the hardest part of Mary's life was that Lincoln's job required him to travel from court to court. She was often left alone for months at a time. Sometimes her nerves frayed and she exploded at him. But he remained patient no matter what her mood was.

"I never saw a more loving couple," said a nephew.

It was an era when the wife was supposed to be the angel in the house. Mary proved she could be that, but she saw herself as more.

"I've become quite a politician," she said, "a rather unladylike profession."

In her quest, Mary was always nagging, cheering, and even bragging: "My husband is going to be the President of the United States one day."

This would make *him* burst out laughing. "But nobody knows me," he would say.

"They soon will," she'd respond.

When Lincoln was elected to Congress in 1846, Mary moved the family to Washington, DC, to be with him. Folks were shocked—it was such a rough town that few women lived there. But Mary didn't care what they thought.

"She wishes to loom largely," said a friend.

But Washington's unpaved streets were full of pigs, human waste, dead animals, and men spitting tobacco. The Lincolns got to see many plays at the theaters, but otherwise Mary was cooped up with two wild boys in her boarding-house room. She lasted several months, more than other wives even tried. Then she took the kids and left Lincoln in his all-male world.

Mary considered herself "a happy, loving, laughing mama." Her parenting style was unusual. She romped with her boys and rarely punished them. Her "angel boys" got elaborate birthday parties with dozens of friends. They could have any pets they wanted—turtles, rats, crows, goats, snakes. In an age when many children died young, she obsessed over their health.

While Lincoln was gone, she relied on her oldest son, Robert, as a companion. They had piano lessons together, went shopping, took trips, and played jokes on each other.

When three-year-old Edward died in 1850, it tore Mary apart. She was weeping too hard to attend the funeral. After a gloomy year, her third son, Willie, was born, followed by Tad.

The family needed more space. In 1856, while Lincoln was away, she added a second story. She paid for it with money her father had left her, and Lincoln left all the decisions to her. She designed the house to be a showcase for Lincoln. She planned parties where people could get to know him over macaroons, her famous white cake, and lots of strawberries.

A visitor said, "You would have known instantly that she who presided over the modest household was a true type

of the American lady"—*exactly* the impression she was going for.

Lincoln considered Mary his chief adviser. When he was offered the governorship of Oregon, it was she who said no. Better that he stay in Illinois and start campaigning for Congress. When he started giving speeches, he read them to her first.

Lincoln's (male) friends were appalled. As he did with everything, he made a joke out of Mary's active role: "I have always found it difficult to make my wife do what she does not want to."

What she wanted never wavered. When he finally ran for president in 1860, she followed him on the campaign trail and gave interviews. Newspapers praised her as "a sparkling talker."

Her dream was within reach, and she couldn't wait.

As soon as he found out the results, Lincoln hurried to tell his wife. "Mary! Mary! We are elected!" he was heard to call. They went out for a victory dinner of sandwiches and coffee and held hands as they walked home.

Abraham Lincoln was now our sixteenth president. And a gleeful Mary Lincoln was now in the national spotlight.

On Inauguration Day, rumors flew that Lincoln would be shot before sundown. He warned women to stay indoors. But Mary refused to leave his side on that dazzling day.

The threats came from Southern leaders who despised

Lincoln's commitment to keeping the country united. Something was looming even more largely than Mary—the Civil War. America was splitting in two.

Mary started breaking rules, even stepping on toes, all over the place. Her first priority was showing that the Lincolns were perfectly proper folks who deserved to be in the White House. The snobby people in Washington were mostly from elite Virginia families. They dubbed Kentucky as "the West" and the Lincolns as "Westerners"—as in wild, rough, uncouth.

"I must dress in costly materials," said Mary. "The people scrutinize every article that I wear with critical curiosity." She hired her own private dressmaker—Elizabeth Keckley—a former slave who had begun sewing the most elegant clothes.

Mary ordered some sixteen new dresses to start, each one more gorgeous than the last, like a white dress with sixty velvet black bows and hundreds of black dots. She favored flamboyantly full skirts, fine fabrics of satin and silk, trims of lace and fur, all adorned with pearls and diamonds, plus fresh flowers in her hair. Lincoln was always saying how charming she looked.

In a relationship daring for its time, Elizabeth became Mary's best friend. While other women in Washington

seemed to treat Mary badly without even knowing her, she felt she could really talk to this strong, successful business-woman.

She kept her husband fed, sending him trays when he worked so long that he forgot to eat. But, ironically, her political power was slipping away.

Lincoln now had lots of male advisers with a strict "no girls allowed" policy. Mary didn't think they were anywhere near as smart and savvy as she was. To them she insisted, "My husband places great faith in my knowledge of human nature." She set about advising Lincoln on whom to pick for his Cabinet, the heads of the various departments of the government.

Lincoln did listen to her at first but concluded she was too critical. If he followed her advice, he'd have a Cabinet of one: Mary. *That* was clearly impossible.

A newspaper scolded, "We have for the first time in the history of presidents, a President's wife who seems to be ambitious of having a finger in the government pie." No one approved: "The American people are so unused to these things, that it is not easy for them to like it."

At least Mary could still organize social functions. But no—that job was turned over to his two male secretaries. When she interfered anyway, they called her names like "her Satanic majesty" and "hellcat."

"Getting more hell-cattical day by day," sniped one.

Some newspapers praised her poise, pointing out that she had more of it than her husband. They hailed her "brilliant flashes of wit." She always kept up her end of the conversation, even when French was required. She did a superb job reviewing the troops when they marched past the White House. She made sure to look soldiers in the eye and engage them, while Lincoln was apt to turn away to murmur with friends.

Later the press turned negative. Many First Ladies get flak no matter what they do. But Mary Lincoln truly couldn't win, especially once the Civil War officially broke out in April 1861.

To Northerners, Mary seemed to be a traitor. After all, she had been born in the South, still spoke with a Southern accent, and had half brothers and other relatives fighting for the South. She was in fact fiercely loyal to the North, so Southerners likewise branded her a traitor.

"I seem to be the scapegoat for both North and South," she observed correctly.

What could she do? She found refuge in the one job open to her—redecorating the embarrassment of a White House.

Willie and Tad thought the White House was the coolest playground ever (Robert was away at college). But it had been neglected for so many years that everything was threadbare, dirty, stained, or broken. The rats outnumbered the pieces of china that matched. Mary believed that a nice White House was important to her husband's prestige, a symbol to prove the Union would endure.

Congress agreed and gave her a budget.

She poured her mighty energy into turning the house into a palace. Said her architect, "She is a smart intelligent woman who likes to have her own way pretty much. I am delighted with her independence."

She modernized the White House with gaslight and running water. She spent madly on the best rugs, furniture, silverware, books, and matching china. She went to extremes, and so did the bills—she ramped them up way over budget.

When Lincoln found out, it was one of the few times he was heard yelling at her. Horrified, he asked how she could splurge on what he called "flub dubs," while his soldiers were going without supplies.

Mary found creative ways to get the bills paid, like begging staff to pad expenses in other departments.

Meanwhile, the war was swallowing up her husband. It was going badly, with a staggering loss of Americans. Instead of savoring cozy evenings, she rarely saw Lincoln before eleven each night.

But in 1862, to show off the improved White House, they threw a huge party with all the best food and wine. The band played a new song called "The Mary Lincoln Polka" while everyone feasted.

The party was a success, but they couldn't enjoy it.

Upstairs their precious son Willie was dying of typhoid fever, and Mary kept leaving the party to sit with him.

After Willie's death, Mary didn't get out of bed for three weeks. She took it as a punishment for her ambition: "I had become so wrapped in the world, so devoted to our political advancement that I thought of little else besides." Her wails could be heard throughout the White House.

People felt sorry for her, but only up to a point. Nearly every family was losing a son to the ghastly Civil War.

Lincoln tried to help her, but it was his job to focus on saving the country.

Mary carried on as best she could. She visited wounded soldiers several times a week—feeding them, writing letters for them. She threw her support into an organization founded by her friend Elizabeth—helping slaves who'd escaped and come to Washington with nothing. Mary donated money, got others to contribute, and went to their camps to hand out blankets and food.

To get relief from painful headaches and other illnesses, she traveled. She took off for months at a time, exploring without a chaperone, visiting museums, and climbing mountains. "Such female vigor," one reporter said with a sniff.

Mary also formed an elite group that met in the Blue

Room to discuss books and current events. She became the first First Lady to welcome African Americans as guests to the White House. She helped women get jobs in the treasury and war departments, as well as jobs as nurses (at a time when nursing was a male job). She pressured Lincoln to keep Robert out of the army as long as possible. After she begged him to pardon a young man who'd deserted the army, Lincoln gave in "by request of the 'Lady President.'"

Historians love to debate about Mary's actual influence

on Lincoln. But most agree that she pushed him toward the Emancipation Proclamation of 1863. It banned slavery in ten states. Most whites opposed it, but not Mary. She called it the end of "the great evil . . . so long allowed to curse the land," and considered it to be a personal victory.

Then she cheered Lincoln on as he led the movement to outlaw slavery in all the states. His biggest triumph came in 1865—doing just that by getting the enormously controversial thirteenth amendment passed in Congress.

Mary also sometimes traveled with Lincoln on visits to the troops in the field. In March 1865, four years into the war, she traveled by carriage to Virginia to see troops while he went ahead by horseback. Everyone's emotions were pitched too high with the endless stress of the war.

When Mary arrived, she was seated at the back, while in the front row a young woman sat next to Lincoln. Mary decided this was shabby treatment of her and made a scene. She shouted at Lincoln, the woman, and those who tried to calm her down. It was the first really public display of her temper since Lincoln had become president. He was mortified, and afterward Mary felt even worse.

The laughter had gone out of their marriage. She worried about the many death threats against him much more than he did. Both were in ill health. He was severely underweight, aging rapidly. She urged him to take rides in their carriage, get to bed earlier, and go to plays and concerts.

At long last, on April 9 the South surrendered, ending the war. The minute Lincoln got the news, he rushed to tell Mary. Four years of hell were over!

She could look forward to something new—being First Lady of a nation at peace. On carriage rides, the couple started chatting about what they would do after his presidency—travel to Europe and California, relax, maybe even laugh again.

"Between the loss of our darling Willie and the war," he told her, "we have both been very miserable. We have to be more cheerful."

Five days after the war ended, Mary held her husband's hand while they enjoyed a comedy at Ford's Theatre. A sudden gunshot exploded right behind them. Lincoln had been shot by one of his many enemies, John Wilkes Booth.

Mary caught her husband in her arms and screamed over and over, "They have shot the president! Why didn't they shoot me?"

She was so hysterical, so in shock, that the men in charge banned her from the room where Lincoln was taken. All that night she was unable to be by his side. He died the following morning at age fifty-six.

As always, Mary was too grief-stricken to go to the funeral. And she refused to see people who came to pay their respects.

Workers built a wooden platform to hold Lincoln's coffin. To Mary, alone in her room, each strike of the hammer was like another bullet from the gun.

Not only had she lost her husband, she had lost her role as "Mrs. President."

Over the next seventeen years Mary picked herself up from one sadness after another. She traveled, shopped, and fought to support herself—and broke enough rules that some became concerned.

Elizabeth remained her closest friend at first. Mary roped her into one of her many attempts to earn money—selling off her fabulous outfits. It turned out nobody wanted them, and the press pounced on this "Old Clothes Scandal." A reporter tsk-tsked that the scheme made "us blush for our country and for our womanhood."

Then, three years after the assassination, Elizabeth published a behind-the-scenes tell-all book about her years in the White House. Deeply hurt, Mary cut Elizabeth out of her life.

Lawyers kept Mary from getting her share of Lincoln's estate for years. When she finally did, she took off to Germany with Tad. "To avoid persecution from the vampire press, I have decided to flee to a land of strangers" was how she explained her bold move.

She asked Congress to grant her an annual pension as the widow of a president. But many of the men there didn't like her. They labeled her "un-American, unfeminine Mary Lincoln . . . indecent." It took years for her to get a pension, and even then she judged it too small.

In 1871, just as she and her son returned to America, Tad died at age eighteen of a lung infection.

"I feel there is no life left to me," said Mary.

More than ever, she was obsessed with money. She would walk around with huge amounts of cash sewn into her clothes. At the same time, she splurged on things she couldn't use, like curtains (when she lived in hotels) and colorful dresses (when she wore only black). She began obsessing over other, odder things. Were people following her, trying to poison her? Did the vice president really have her husband murdered?

One morning, ten years after her husband's assassination, two policemen and a lawyer showed up in her hotel room. Robert, the only son she had left, was having her arrested.

Robert was in a tough spot. He found the bad publicity she attracted embarrassing, and he also genuinely feared for her safety. All he could think of was to have her put away somewhere, like a mental hospital. It was still a time when it was not hard for men to shut away women just for being in the way.

Later that day Mary was brought to court. A parade of witnesses spoke against her. They said things such as: "She was not like ladies in general." Robert cried several times during the trial but concluded, "I have no doubt my mother is insane."

Mental illness was poorly understood then. Ever since, scholars have debated furiously about whether Mary had one and what it might have been.

Once at the hospital, she handled the humiliation with real courage. Immediately she began crafting her escape. She had letters smuggled out to the exact person who could help: one of the few women lawyers in the United States and an advocate for women's rights.

Mary was free within four months. She dusted herself off and moved to France.

Her health declined after she suffered injuries in a fall. She spent her final years with her sister in Springfield. Not long after forgiving Robert, she died on July 16, 1882, after a stroke. She was sixty-three.

Mary Lincoln's reputation suffered and her place in history was neglected for a while. But today she fascinates historians, storytellers, and moviemakers. Everyone argues about her. Was she the worst First Lady in history? Or the most significant? Could she have been a president herself? Was she a victim, a villain, or just ahead of her time?

"Search the world over, and you will not find her counterpart," said the one who perhaps knew her best, her former friend Elizabeth.

There was simply no one like Mary Lincoln.

★ SOURCES AND FURTHER READING ★

Books
(* especially for young readers)

Baker, Jean H. *Mary Todd Lincoln: A Biography*. New York: Norton, 1987.

Clinton, Catherine. *Mrs. Lincoln: A Life*. New York: HarperCollins, 2010.

Emerson, Jason. *The Madness of Mary Lincoln*. Carbondale, IL: Southern Illinois University Press, 2007.

Epstein, Daniel Mark. *The Lincolns: Portrait of a Marriage*. New York: Ballantine, 2008.

Fleischner, Jennifer. *Mrs. Lincoln and Mrs. Keckly: The Remarkable Story of the Friendship between a First Lady and a Former Slave*. New York: Broadway Books, 2003.

* Fleming, Candace. *The Lincolns: A Scrapbook Look at Abraham and Mary*. New York: Schwartz & Wade, 2008.

* Jones, Lynda. *Mrs. Lincoln's Dressmaker: The Unlikely Friendship of Elizabeth Keckley and Mary Todd Lincoln*. Washington, DC: National Geographic, 2009.

Keckley, Elizabeth. *Behind the Scenes: Or, Thirty Years a Slave, and Four Years in the White House*. New York: Oxford University Press, 1988.

* Krull, Kathleen, and Paul Brewer. *Lincoln Tells a Joke: How Laughter Saved the President (and the Country)*. Boston: Harcourt, 2010.

* Larkin, Tanya. *What Was Cooking in Mary Todd Lincoln's White House?* New York: PowerKids Press, 2001.

Truman, Margaret. *First Ladies*. New York: Random House, 1995.

Williams, Frank J., and Michael Burkhimer, eds. *The Mary Lincoln Enigma: Historians on America's Most Controversial First Lady*. Carbondale, IL: Southern Illinois University Press, 2012.

Websites

Abraham and Mary Lincoln: A House Divided, PBS's American Experience:
www.pbs.org/wgbh/americanexperience/films/lincolns

Lincoln Home National Historic Site: **www.nps.gov/liho**

Mary Lincoln, C-Span's "First Ladies: Influence and Image":
firstladies.c-span.org/FirstLady/18/Mary-Lincoln.aspx

Mary Todd Lincoln House: **www.mtlhouse.org**

Mary Todd Lincoln Research Site: **rogerjnorton.com/Lincoln15.html**

National First Ladies' Library: **www.firstladies.org**

★ INDEX ★